# Slay Your Day

*Journal*

*The Official Companion to the Best-Selling Book*

## Sandi Glandt

# Dedication

To my J Crew—Jarrod, Jacob, and Jordan—you are my sun, my moon, and every single star in my sky. You are the light that guides me, the reason I strive to be the best I can be every single day, and the anchor that keeps me grounded. Because of you, I get to live as the very best version of myself. Everything I do is rooted in being the best wife and mama I can possibly be to you three. Thank you for your love, your patience, your laughter, your endless snuggles and cuddles, and for always believing in me. Being your wife and mama is, and will forever be, the greatest gift of my life. G-d has truly blessed us beyond measure.

And to every woman who has ever wondered *"Can I really have it all?"* The answer is hands down, unequivocally YES. Not only can you have it all, but you have the power to create it all—on your terms, in your own beautiful blueprint. May you fill your days with love, laughter, purpose, and the courage to live out your wildest dreams.

# Table of Contents

# How to Use This Journal

This is your sacred space.

Welcome to your *Slay Your Day* Companion Journal, your daily tool for creating a life by design, not by default. Inspired by the teachings of *Slay Your Day*, this journal is designed to help you embody the energy, clarity, and confidence of a high-performing woman who knows what she wants and isn't afraid to claim it.

Here, you will meet yourself. The real you. The you with dreams, visions, desires, and goals too important to ignore. Each day, you'll be guided through prompts that challenge you to reflect, release, recalibrate, and RISE. This is more than journaling. This is a container of transformation.

Each prompt is designed to:

- Support you in shifting out of overwhelm and into alignment.
- Connect you to your purpose and remind you of your power.
- Hold you accountable to your daily intentions and actions.
- Give you a safe space to dream bigger, work smarter, and slay harder.

**Let's Get Practical:**

- This journal follows the order of chapters in *Slay Your Day*. Start with Chapter 1. Read it. Let it sink in. Then open to Day 1 of this journal and begin.
- You'll find an inspiring quote and one journaling prompt per day. Each prompt is meant to guide you into deeper thought and purposeful action.
- You can write morning or night, or whenever you need to reconnect.
- Don't worry about writing the "right" thing. There is no right. There is only *real*.
- Miss a day? That's OK. Come back. Pick up where you left off. Your journey is yours to own.

Your only job is to keep showing up for YOU.

This journal is for the woman who is ready to:

- Step into her next-level self.
- Design her days with clarity and confidence.
- Stop surviving and start slaying.

Let this be your mirror, your motivator, your mindset reset.

You already have what it takes.

Now … let's slay your day—one page, one prompt, one breakthrough at a time.

I love you.

xo,

Sandi Glandt

"Your breakdown is not your ending—it's your awakening."

— Sandi Glandt

"Rock bottom became the solid foundation
on which I rebuilt my life."
— J. K. Rowling

# Chapter 1: Breakdowns Bring Breakthroughs

Welcome to the first chapter of your journaling journey, **Breakdowns Bring Breakthroughs**. This section is all about honoring your story—especially the moments that felt like everything was falling apart. These pages are a space for you to reflect on the seasons that broke you open, and uncover the wisdom, strength, and purpose that came from them.

Before each journaling session, take a deep breath. Let go of judgment. Know that whatever you feel, remember, or discover is valid and important. Let this be a sacred space to reconnect with your truth. Write with honesty. Write with grace. And write knowing that every reflection brings you one step closer to the breakthrough you deserve.

1. **Describe a time in your life that felt like rock bottom.**
   What emotions came up for you in that season?

   _____

   _____

   _____

   _____

   _____

   _____

   _____

   _____

   _____

   _____

   _____

   _____

   _____

2. **What did you discover about yourself in your breakdown moment?**
What truths were revealed?

_____

_____

_____

_____

_____

_____

_____

_____

_____

_____

_____

_____

_____

3. **When did you realize your "breakdown" was actually the beginning of something new?** Describe that turning point.

_____

_____

_____

_____

_____

_____

_____

_____

_____

_____

_____

_____

4. **What helped you begin the process of reclaiming yourself and your power?**

_____

_____

_____

_____

_____

_____

_____

_____

_____

_____

_____

_____

_____

5. **What does your "new normal" look like today, and how does it differ from before?**

_____

_____

_____

_____

_____

_____

_____

_____

_____

_____

_____

_____

_____

6. **What daily habits or micro-wins helped you rebuild your confidence and momentum?**

_____

_____

_____

_____

_____

_____

_____

_____

_____

_____

_____

_____

7. **List three things you do now that your past overwhelmed self would be proud of.**

_____

_____

_____

_____

_____

_____

_____

_____

_____

_____

_____

_____

_____

8. **Write out your three overarching goals for today. Why are these your non-negotiables?**

_____

_____

_____

_____

_____

_____

_____

_____

_____

_____

_____

_____

_____

9. **What systems or routines can you put in place to support your daily wins?**

_____

_____

_____

_____

_____

_____

_____

_____

_____

_____

_____

_____

_____

10. **What message would your future self give you about the power of this season you're in?**

_____

_____

_____

_____

_____

_____

_____

_____

_____

_____

_____

_____

_____

"The woman you want to become is already inside you. She's just waiting for you to show up and lead."

— Sandi Glandt

"You don't become what you want. You become what you believe."

— Oprah Winfrey

# Chapter 2: Helping Success-Minded Women Be the Best Versions of Themselves

This chapter is all about clarity, commitment, and stepping into your personal power. As you reflect on this part of your journey, you're invited to get real about what you want, what's been holding you back, and what needs to shift so you can fully become the version of you that already exists within.

These prompts will help you clarify your mission, embody your highest potential, and uncover what it takes to move from overwhelmed to empowered. This is where you stop wishing and start walking in the direction of your goals—with purpose, focus, and fire.

Breathe in belief. Breathe out excuses. Let's do this.

1. **What does the "best version" of you look like, feel like, and operate like?**
   Describe her in vivid detail.

   _____

   _____

   _____

   _____

   _____

   _____

   _____

   _____

   _____

   _____

   _____

   _____

   _____

2. **What parts of your current life are not aligned with the version of you that you're stepping into?**

_____

_____

_____

_____

_____

_____

_____

_____

_____

_____

_____

_____

_____

3.  **What are three excuses or limiting beliefs you've told yourself in the past that are no longer allowed?**

_____

_____

_____

_____

_____

_____

_____

_____

_____

_____

_____

_____

4.  **What would it look like for you to show up as the CEO of your life today?**

_____

_____

_____

_____

_____

_____

_____

_____

_____

_____

_____

_____

5. **What systems, routines, or structures could you implement this week to support your growth?**

_____

_____

_____

_____

_____

_____

_____

_____

_____

_____

_____

_____

6. **What's one area of your life that feels disorganized or overwhelming—and what is one small step you can take today to shift it?**

_____

_____

_____

_____

_____

_____

_____

_____

_____

_____

_____

_____

7. **How would your family, business, or well-being change if you fully committed to this journey?**

_____

_____

_____

_____

_____

_____

_____

_____

_____

_____

_____

_____

_____

8. **What do you need to forgive yourself for so you can move forward with power?**

_____

_____

_____

_____

_____

_____

_____

_____

_____

_____

_____

_____

9. **What would it look like to *decide*—right now—that you are no longer available for burnout, stress, or chaos?**

_____

_____

_____

_____

_____

_____

_____

_____

_____

_____

_____

_____

10. **Write a commitment letter to yourself. Who are you becoming, and what are you now claiming as your new standard?**

_____

_____

_____

_____

_____

_____

_____

_____

_____

_____

_____

_____

_____

"You don't need more time. You need more clarity on what matters."
— Sandi Glandt

"It's not about doing more, it's about doing what matters most."

— Greg McKeown, Essentialism

# Chapter 3: Trading Overwhelm for Purpose

This chapter is your permission slip to drop the overwhelm and live on purpose—every single day. Overwhelm thrives where intention is absent. But once you take back your schedule, get clear on your top priorities, and begin focusing on wins (not never-ending to-dos), everything shifts.

This section is designed to help you simplify your focus, celebrate small victories, and align your energy with what truly matters. Instead of chasing productivity, you'll learn how to anchor into purpose—so that every task, decision, and commitment feels aligned with your best self.

Use these prompts to gain clarity, make empowered decisions, and set yourself up to slay your day from a place of calm and confidence.

1. **What does it look and feel like when you're living your day with purpose, not panic?**

_____

_____

_____

_____

_____

_____

_____

_____

_____

_____

_____

2. **List your three most important goals for today. How will achieving these help you feel accomplished?**

_____

_____

_____

_____

_____

_____

_____

_____

_____

_____

_____

_____

3. **What wins did you already have today—even the small ones? Celebrate them here.**

_____

_____

_____

_____

_____

_____

_____

_____

_____

_____

_____

_____

4. **What is one thing on your plate that's causing unnecessary stress and can be deleted, delegated, or delayed?**

_____

_____

_____

_____

_____

_____

_____

_____

_____

_____

_____

5. **Describe a time when you felt completely in flow. What contributed to that feeling?**

_____

_____

_____

_____

_____

_____

_____

_____

_____

_____

_____

_____

_____

6. **Where do you feel resistance or chaos in your daily life? What might it be trying to teach you?**

---

---

---

---

---

---

---

---

---

---

---

---

7. **What does your ideal daily schedule look like—and how does it support your purpose?**

_____

_____

_____

_____

_____

_____

_____

_____

_____

_____

_____

_____

8. **How can you better protect your energy and focus throughout your day?**

_____

_____

_____

_____

_____

_____

_____

_____

_____

_____

_____

_____

9. **What boundaries do you need to put in place this week to trade overwhelm for peace?**

_____

_____

_____

_____

_____

_____

_____

_____

_____

_____

_____

_____

10. **Finish this sentence: When I live with purpose, I feel _____.**

"Your time is not a renewable resource.
Spend it wisely."

— Sandi Glandt

"Show me your calendar, and I'll show you your priorities."

— James Clear

# Chapter 4: How Much Is Your Time Worth?

Time is your most valuable resource—and yet, it's the one we often give away the fastest. In this chapter, we're getting honest about how you spend your time, who or what gets the best of your energy, and how you can take back control to create more freedom, focus, and fulfillment.

This is your chance to redefine what "balance" looks like for you. To become the kind of woman who protects her time like she protects her peace. These prompts will guide you to evaluate what's helping you move forward, what's holding you back, and how to start showing up for your life with more intention.

When you know what your time is worth, you stop giving it away to things that don't align with your values, goals, or purpose. Let's get clear on what matters—so you can slay your day with power and purpose.

1. **Describe your current relationship with time. Do you feel in control of it—or does it control you?**

_____

_____

_____

_____

_____

_____

_____

_____

_____

_____

_____

_____

2. **If your time was money, what areas of your life are currently giving you the best return on investment (ROI)? Which are draining you?**

_____

_____

_____

_____

_____

_____

_____

_____

_____

_____

_____

3. **Write out what your ideal day looks like—from the moment you wake up to the moment you go to bed.**

_____

_____

_____

_____

_____

_____

_____

_____

_____

_____

_____

_____

4. **Compare your ideal day to your current day. What are the biggest gaps, and what's one small step you can take to close them?**

_____

_____

_____

_____

_____

_____

_____

_____

_____

_____

_____

_____

_____

5. **What are your top three money-making moves or high-impact activities in your business/life right now?**

_____

_____

_____

_____

_____

_____

_____

_____

_____

_____

_____

_____

6. **List the top three time-suckers or energy-drainers you know you need to eliminate, delegate, or restructure.**

_____

_____

_____

_____

_____

_____

_____

_____

_____

_____

_____

7. **What is one boundary you can set this week to protect your time and energy?**

_____

_____

_____

_____

_____

_____

_____

_____

_____

_____

_____

_____

8. **How can you use the S.M.A.R.T. framework (Specific, Measurable, Attainable, Realistic, Timely) to get closer to one of your current goals?**

_____

_____

_____

_____

_____

_____

_____

_____

_____

_____

_____

_____

9. **Where in your life do you feel "guilt" when it comes to how you spend your time (e.g., mom guilt, business guilt, self-care guilt)? What would it feel like to release that?**

_____

_____

_____

_____

_____

_____

_____

_____

_____

_____

_____

_____

_____

10. **Finish this sentence: "When I honor my time, I feel**

_____."

Let that word guide how you design your day moving

forward.

"If you don't prioritize your life.
someone else will."

— Greg McKeown. *Essentialism*

"Protecting your time is how you protect your energy, your goals, and your greatness."

— Sandi Glandt

# Chapter 5: Protect Your Time

Time doesn't just disappear—you give it away. And the truth is, if you don't protect your time, someone else will fill it for you.

This chapter is your wake-up call to treat time like the valuable currency it is. You'll learn how to identify time-suckers, stop multitasking, and take back control of your daily hours with confidence. Because when you protect your time, you protect your peace, your priorities, and your potential.

These prompts will help you break old habits, eliminate distractions, and implement systems to streamline your schedule. You'll discover how much more energy and focus you have when you're intentional about every hour of your day.

No more living by default. It's time to design your day—and protect it like the powerhouse woman you are.

1. **What does protecting your time mean to you—and what would it look like if you actually did it daily?**

_____

_____

_____

_____

_____

_____

_____

_____

_____

_____

_____

_____

_____

2. **Track your last twenty-four hours: Where did your time go? What surprised you? What drained you?**

_____

_____

_____

_____

_____

_____

_____

_____

_____

_____

_____

_____

3. **What is one time-sucker you know you need to eliminate immediately to get closer to your goals?**

_____

_____

_____

_____

_____

_____

_____

_____

_____

_____

_____

_____

4. **Write out your "ideal week" with themed days and batching strategies. How would it change your energy and output?**

_____

_____

_____

_____

_____

_____

_____

_____

_____

_____

_____

_____

5. **Which daily habits or patterns tend to pull you off track (think: phone scrolling, interruptions, procrastination)? How can you shift them?**

_____

_____

_____

_____

_____

_____

_____

_____

_____

_____

_____

_____

6. **Which of your current tasks fall into each of these categories:**

- Urgent & Important
- Important but Not Urgent
- Urgent but Not Important
- Neither Urgent nor Important

_____

_____

_____

_____

_____

_____

_____

_____

_____

_____

_____

_____

7. **How do distractions show up in your day, and what systems can you put in place to minimize them?**

_____

_____

_____

_____

_____

_____

_____

_____

_____

_____

_____

_____

8.  **If you gained an extra hour each day by eliminating time-suckers, what would you use that time for?**

_____

_____

_____

_____

_____

_____

_____

_____

_____

_____

_____

9. **What boundaries do you need to set (with yourself or others) to stay focused and in flow?**

_____

_____

_____

_____

_____

_____

_____

_____

_____

_____

_____

_____

_____

10. **What does being the CEO of your time look and feel like? Describe it in detail.**

_____

_____

_____

_____

_____

_____

_____

_____

_____

_____

_____

_____

"When you say 'yes' to others, make sure you're not saying 'no' to yourself."
— Paulo Coelho

"Your nonnegotiables are your power. When you honor them, you teach the world how to treat you."

— Sandi Glandt

# Chapter 6: Know Your Nonnegotiables

How often do you say yes when you really want to say no? If you're like most women, the answer is "too often."

This chapter is about taking your power back—by identifying your personal nonnegotiables. These are the boundaries, values, and priorities that define what you say yes to, what you walk away from, and how you show up in every area of your life. When you get clear on what matters most to you, decision-making becomes easier, guilt fades away, and alignment becomes your new normal.

These prompts will guide you in mapping out your YES and NO lists, so you can stop people-pleasing and start protecting your peace. This is your permission slip to stop over-explaining and start honoring your time, energy, and values.

Say yes to what serves your soul. Say no to what doesn't. You're allowed.

1. **What does the phrase *nonnegotiable* mean to you, and why is it important in your life right now?**

_____

_____

_____

_____

_____

_____

_____

_____

_____

_____

_____

_____

2.  **Make a list of your top five nonnegotiables. Why are these priorities essential to your happiness and success?**

_____

_____

_____

_____

_____

_____

_____

_____

_____

_____

_____

_____

3. **What is one area of your life where you've been saying yes too much and it's left you feeling resentful or burnt out?**

_____

_____

_____

_____

_____

_____

_____

_____

_____

_____

_____

_____

4. **Where have you compromised your own boundaries or values to make others more comfortable? How did it feel?**

_____

_____

_____

_____

_____

_____

_____

_____

_____

_____

_____

_____

5. **What limiting beliefs (like guilt or fear of disappointing others) have stopped you from enforcing your nonnegotiables?**

_____

_____

_____

_____

_____

_____

_____

_____

_____

_____

_____

_____

6. **Write out your personal YES list. What lights you up, energizes you, or aligns with your core values?**

_____

_____

_____

_____

_____

_____

_____

_____

_____

_____

_____

_____

7. **Now write your NO list. What drains you, pulls you out of alignment, or doesn't serve your highest self anymore?**

_____

_____

_____

_____

_____

_____

_____

_____

_____

_____

_____

_____

8. **Describe a situation where you honored a nonnegotiable. What was the outcome? How did you feel?**

_____

_____

_____

_____

_____

_____

_____

_____

_____

_____

_____

_____

9. **How can you start saying no with more confidence and less guilt? Write out a go-to phrase to help you set a boundary with grace.**

_____

_____

_____

_____

_____

_____

_____

_____

_____

_____

_____

_____

_____

10. **Imagine your ideal life. What boundaries need to be in place for you to create and protect that life with ease?**

_____

_____

_____

_____

_____

_____

_____

_____

_____

_____

_____

_____

"If you want to go fast, go alone. If you want to go far, go together. Delegate to elevate."

— African proverb

"You don't have to do everything. You just have to do the right things."

— Sandi Glandt

# Chapter 7: The 3D System to Step into Success

Success doesn't happen by accident—it happens by design. And one of the most powerful tools for designing your life is the 3D System: **Do It, Delegate It, or Delete It**. This chapter is about simplifying your days so you can create more space for what matters most.

You're not meant to do it all. You're meant to do the right things—the ones that align with your purpose, bring in results, and allow you to show up with joy. When you implement this system, you stop spinning your wheels and start making real progress in your business, relationships, and personal growth.

These prompts will help you brain-dump everything on your plate and place each item into one of the three D's. Use this exercise to realign your energy, free up mental space, and step into success on *your* terms.

1.  **What does success look and feel like for you in this season of life? Be specific about how you want your days to feel and flow.**

_____

_____

_____

_____

_____

_____

_____

_____

_____

_____

_____

2. **What are the three to five tasks that only YOU can do in your life or business? Why are these so important to protect?**

_____

_____

_____

_____

_____

_____

_____

_____

_____

_____

_____

_____

3. **List five things you are currently doing that someone else could do just as well—or better. What would delegating these free up for you?**

_____

_____

_____

_____

_____

_____

_____

_____

_____

_____

_____

_____

4. **What fears or limiting beliefs come up when you think about delegating tasks to others? Where did those beliefs come from?**

_____

_____

_____

_____

_____

_____

_____

_____

_____

_____

_____

_____

5. **If you could wave a magic wand and delete three tasks, obligations, or time-sucks from your life, what would they be?**

_____

_____

_____

_____

_____

_____

_____

_____

_____

_____

_____

_____

6. **What task are you currently doing that feels heavy, low ROI, or misaligned with your version of success? Which D does it fall under?**

_____

_____

_____

_____

_____

_____

_____

_____

_____

_____

_____

_____

7. **What area of your business or personal life would benefit most from the 3D System right now? Why?**

_____

_____

_____

_____

_____

_____

_____

_____

_____

_____

_____

_____

8. **What's one small task you can delegate or delete THIS WEEK to start taking back your time and energy?**

_____

_____

_____

_____

_____

_____

_____

_____

_____

_____

_____

_____

9. **How does it feel when you give yourself permission to *not* do it all? What opens up for you mentally, emotionally, and creatively?**

_____

_____

_____

_____

_____

_____

_____

_____

_____

_____

_____

_____

10. **After reviewing your Do, Delegate, and Delete lists, what's one boundary you need to put in place to protect your new priorities?**

_____

_____

_____

_____

_____

_____

_____

_____

_____

_____

_____

"For every minute spent organizing, an hour is earned."

— Benjamin Franklin

"Clutter is not just physical stuff. It's old ideas, toxic relationships, and bad habits. Clutter is anything that does not support your better self."

— Eleanor Brownn

# Chapter 8: Organizing Home & Work

If your space is cluttered, your mind will be too. Organization isn't just about aesthetics—it's about setting yourself up to succeed. Whether it's your kitchen counter, your desktop, or your daily calendar, everything around you either supports or disrupts your flow.

When your home and work life are organized, you feel more in control, focused, and calm. You save time, energy, and even money. But most importantly, you step into your power as a woman who knows how to manage her environment with grace and intention.

This section is designed to help you identify the areas where you need structure, so you can reclaim your peace of mind. Use these prompts to declutter your spaces and your thoughts—and build a sustainable system that supports your productivity and purpose.

1. **How does your current environment—home or workspace—affect your mood and productivity on a daily basis? Be honest.**

_____

_____

_____

_____

_____

_____

_____

_____

_____

_____

_____

_____

2. **What's one area of your home or office that instantly stresses you out when it's messy? What would it feel like to have that space clean and organized?**

_____

_____

_____

_____

_____

_____

_____

_____

_____

_____

_____

_____

3. **Which part of your home or workspace do you want to tackle first? What's your *why* behind starting there?**

_____

_____

_____

_____

_____

_____

_____

_____

_____

_____

_____

_____

_____

4. **Think about your daily routine: What organizational habit could save you time, reduce stress, or help you show up more powerfully?**

_____

_____

_____

_____

_____

_____

_____

_____

_____

_____

_____

_____

_____

Slay Your Day Journal Prompts

5. **What clutter (physical or digital) is distracting you or slowing you down? How can you begin to simplify it?**

_____

_____

_____

_____

_____

_____

_____

_____

_____

_____

_____

_____

131

6. **Where do things tend to pile up in your home or office? What system can you create to prevent this from happening again?**

_____

_____

_____

_____

_____

_____

_____

_____

_____

_____

_____

_____

7. **What's your ideal "welcome station" or daily drop zone? What would make it beautiful, practical, and efficient for your family?**

_____

_____

_____

_____

_____

_____

_____

_____

_____

_____

_____

_____

8. **What are three habits you can adopt daily or weekly to maintain a cleaner, more organized space?**

_____

_____

_____

_____

_____

_____

_____

_____

_____

_____

_____

_____

9. **What distractions steal your time the most while working at home? How can you create stronger boundaries or systems around them?**

_____

_____

_____

_____

_____

_____

_____

_____

_____

_____

_____

_____

10. **Describe how you'll feel once your home and work life are both in flow and organized. What will that version of you be able to do, feel, and create?**

_____

_____

_____

_____

_____

_____

_____

_____

_____

_____

_____

_____

"You had the power all along,
my dear."
— Glenda the Good Witch.
The Wizard of Oz

"Decide what kind of life you really want ... then say no to everything that isn't that."

— Unknown

# Chapter 9: Take Back Control

You don't need more hours in the day. You need more *intention* behind how you use the ones you already have.

This chapter is all about reclaiming your power—one decision, one boundary, one action step at a time. When you take back control of your time and energy, you begin to operate from a place of purpose rather than chaos. You no longer feel like you're playing catch-up in life; instead, you're leading it.

Use these prompts to evaluate where you've been giving your power away—through procrastination, distraction, toxic habits, or people-pleasing—and map out the habits, boundaries, and daily shifts that will put you back in the driver's seat of your life.

This is your permission slip to stop waiting for things to change and start creating the change yourself.

1. **What is one area of your life that currently feels out of your control? What emotions come up when you think about it?**

_____

_____

_____

_____

_____

_____

_____

_____

_____

_____

_____

_____

_____

2. **What would it look and feel like to be fully in control of that area? Describe your ideal outcome and how you would show up differently.**

_____

_____

_____

_____

_____

_____

_____

_____

_____

_____

_____

3. **Where in your life are you giving your time or energy to things that no longer serve your goals or well-being?**

_____

_____

_____

_____

_____

_____

_____

_____

_____

_____

_____

_____

4. **What distractions or habits do you know are stealing your time each day? What boundaries can you set to limit or remove them?**

_____

_____

_____

_____

_____

_____

_____

_____

_____

_____

_____

_____

5. **In what ways do you currently procrastinate, and what's really behind it—fear, perfectionism, burnout, something else?**

_____

_____

_____

_____

_____

_____

_____

_____

_____

_____

_____

_____

6. **What does "living life on your terms" mean to you? Be bold. Be honest.**

_____

_____

_____

_____

_____

_____

_____

_____

_____

_____

_____

_____

7. **What new habit, ritual, or schedule tweak could you implement this week to take back control of your time and energy?**

_____

_____

_____

_____

_____

_____

_____

_____

_____

_____

_____

_____

8. **Who or what do you need to say no to more often to protect your peace and priorities?**

_____

_____

_____

_____

_____

_____

_____

_____

_____

_____

_____

_____

9. **How does it feel to realize that you already have the power to change your life? What thoughts or beliefs need to shift for you to step into that power daily?**

_____

_____

_____

_____

_____

_____

_____

_____

_____

_____

_____

_____

_____

10. **What is one action step you will take TODAY to take back control of your time, mindset, or surroundings? How will you hold yourself accountable?**

_____

_____

_____

_____

_____

_____

_____

_____

_____

_____

_____

_____

"You can have it all. Just not all at once. And not without intention."
— Sandi Glandt

"There is no force more powerful than a woman determined to rise."

— W.E.B. Dubois (attributed)

# Chapter 10: Claiming Your Power as a Woman Who Wants to HAVE IT ALL

You've done the work. You've implemented the systems. You've upgraded your mindset, your schedule, your habits, and your vision. Now, it's time to *own it*.

This chapter is about unapologetically claiming your power as a woman who wants to have it all—and knows she's worthy of it. But "having it all" doesn't mean doing it all. It means living a life aligned with your values, goals, and deepest desires. It means fulfillment on your terms.

There's no one-size-fits-all version of success or happiness. That's the beauty of it. You get to decide what having it all means for you—and then take aligned action every day to live that truth out loud.

These prompts are designed to help you clarify your personal definition of success, release perfectionism, step fully into your power, and create a life of freedom, flow, and fulfillment. Let's go!

1. **What does "having it all" truly mean to you right now? List out what a fulfilled life looks like in this season.**

_____

_____

_____

_____

_____

_____

_____

_____

_____

_____

_____

_____

2. **What stories, beliefs, or fears have made you feel like you *can't* have it all? Are they really true? Who do they belong to?**

_____

_____

_____

_____

_____

_____

_____

_____

_____

_____

_____

_____

3. **What areas of your life feel most aligned right now—and what areas are asking for more attention or intention?**

_____

_____

_____

_____

_____

_____

_____

_____

_____

_____

_____

_____

_____

4. **If you fully stepped into your power today, how would you speak, move, lead, create, or show up differently?**

_____

_____

_____

_____

_____

_____

_____

_____

_____

_____

_____

5. **What is one bold action you can take this week to move closer to your dream life and step further into your power?**

_____

_____

_____

_____

_____

_____

_____

_____

_____

_____

_____

_____

6.  **What does the most confident, fulfilled version of you believe about herself? How can you embody that belief right now?**

_____

_____

_____

_____

_____

_____

_____

_____

_____

_____

_____

_____

7. **What support systems (people, tools, services) do you need to allow in, so you don't have to do everything alone?**

_____

_____

_____

_____

_____

_____

_____

_____

_____

_____

_____

_____

8. **Where can you let go of perfectionism and allow "good enough" to be powerful and freeing?**

_____

_____

_____

_____

_____

_____

_____

_____

_____

_____

_____

_____

9. **What boundaries do you need to establish or enforce to protect your energy and your vision of having it all?**

_____

_____

_____

_____

_____

_____

_____

_____

_____

_____

_____

_____

**10. How can you intentionally prioritize your buckets— Family, Work, Personal—each day to feel balanced, fulfilled, and unstoppable?**

_____

_____

_____

_____

_____

_____

_____

_____

_____

_____

_____

"Be the girl who decided to go for it."

— Unknown

"*Action is the foundational key to all success.*"

— Pablo Picasso

# Chapter 11: Slay Your Day Today and Every Day

This is it—the final step in your Slay Your Day journey. You've read the insights. You've learned the tools. You've visualized the life you want. Now? It's time to *act*.

This chapter is your permission slip, pep talk, and playbook all wrapped in one. Because the truth is, all the knowledge and intention in the world won't move the needle unless you *move*. Action creates momentum. It builds confidence. It reveals what works, what doesn't, and what's possible for you when you stop waiting and start doing.

You don't need to be perfect. You just need to be consistent. Every time you show up for yourself—no matter how small the step—you prove you're the kind of woman who slays her day and builds her dream life one intentional move at a time.

This final set of journal prompts is designed to help you take that step. Today. Right now. Again tomorrow. And the next day. And the next. Because when you stack up daily wins, you become unstoppable.

1.  **What's the ONE area of your life or business where you're ready to take bold action today? What has been holding you back?**

_____

_____

_____

_____

_____

_____

_____

_____

_____

_____

_____

_____

2. **What small action can you take *immediately* to build momentum toward your next big goal?**

_____

_____

_____

_____

_____

_____

_____

_____

_____

_____

_____

3. **What systems or tools from this book do you want to implement consistently starting this week?**

_____

_____

_____

_____

_____

_____

_____

_____

_____

_____

_____

4. **What limiting belief do you need to release so you can fully step into your power?**

_____

_____

_____

_____

_____

_____

_____

_____

_____

_____

_____

_____

5. **Think of a recent block or challenge—what lesson did it reveal to you, and how can you grow from it now?**

_____

_____

_____

_____

_____

_____

_____

_____

_____

_____

_____

_____

6.  **What's one habit you can build or return to that will move you closer to the woman you want to be?**

_____

_____

_____

_____

_____

_____

_____

_____

_____

_____

_____

7. **What does your next-level self do differently in her day-to-day life? How can you embody that today?**

_____

_____

_____

_____

_____

_____

_____

_____

_____

_____

_____

_____

8. **What's one area where fear is keeping you small? What action can you take to FACE EVERYTHING AND RISE?**

_____

_____

_____

_____

_____

_____

_____

_____

_____

_____

_____

_____

9. **What did you do *right* today? Celebrate your wins—big or small. How did they make you feel?**

_____

_____

_____

_____

_____

_____

_____

_____

_____

_____

_____

_____

10. **What are three things you will do *this week* to stay committed to slaying your day and building your dream life?**

_____

_____

_____

_____

_____

_____

_____

_____

_____

_____

_____

_____

*One Final Prompt to close out your journaling:*

11. **"If I fully stepped into my power starting today, with no excuses and no limits, what would my life look like one year from now?"**

_____

_____

_____

_____

_____

_____

_____

_____

_____

_____

_____

_____

_____

_____

_____

_____

_____

_____

_____

_____

_____

_____

_____

_____

_____

# Final Note to You, the Reader

As you turn the last page of this journey, I want to pause and remind you of something important: **You are already further ahead than you realize.**

The fact that you picked up this book, journaled through these prompts, or gave yourself the space to think differently about your time, your systems, and your life—means you've already chosen growth. You've already chosen yourself. And that alone is worth celebrating.

**Reflection: Look at How Far You've Come**

Think back to the moment you first started this. Maybe you were searching for clarity. Maybe you were juggling more than felt humanly possible. Maybe you simply knew there had to be a better way to live, work, and lead without losing yourself in the process.

Now, here you are—with new tools, fresh insights, and a reminder that you don't have to keep running on empty. You've seen how structure creates freedom, how habits multiply your results, and how putting systems in place gives you back the one resource you can never get back—your time.

You've grown. You've shifted. You've awakened a new level of awareness about what's possible for you.

**This Is Just the Beginning**

It's the beginning of the next chapter of your story.

The systems, strategies, and mindset shifts you've started here are stepping stones into something bigger: the life and business you were created to lead. You don't have to wait until "someday" or the "perfect time." You can start living it *now*.

And yes, there will still be hard days. There will still be distractions, doubts, and detours. But you've built the muscle of resilience. You know now that when things feel overwhelming, you have the ability to pause, reset, and rise again.

**Call to Action: Step into Your Next Level**

So, here's my challenge to you: Don't let this book be the thing that sits pretty on your shelf. Let it be the thing that changes the way you live, work, and show up—for yourself, your family, your clients, your purpose.

- **Pick one system you've learned here and implement it this week.** Start small, but start.
- **Choose one area of your life where you'll no longer settle for survival mode.** Put a plan in place to thrive.
- **Take one bold step toward the vision that's been tugging at your heart.** Don't wait until January. Don't wait until "someday." Your time is now.

Momentum is built one decision, one system, one action at a time.

**An Invitation to Connect**

Finally, I want you to know this: You don't have to do it alone.

The reason I created my programs, my podcast, my events, and this book is because I know the power of community. Transformation happens faster when we do it together.

So, if you're ready for accountability, support, and a roadmap to keep you moving forward—I'd love to connect with you:

✦ **Join me inside my High Performance Academy**, where ambitious women learn how to systemize their life and business in just a few focused hours a day.

✦ **Subscribe to my podcast, *Slay Your Day*,** for weekly strategies, mindset shifts, and real talk about what it takes to thrive as a high-performing woman.

✦ **Follow me on Instagram (@SandiGlandt)**, for daily behind-the-scenes, inspiration, and practical tips you can put into action immediately.

✦ **Attend one of my live events**, because nothing compares to being in the room, surrounded by powerhouse women who are rising together.

My inbox is always open, my DMs are always welcome, and my heart is always cheering you on.

**Final Thought**

You were never meant to simply "get through" your days. You were meant to *slay them.*

So, take what you've learned here and live it. Show up with intention. Build the systems that free you. Lead with confidence. And never forget—your life, your business, your family, your purpose—they all get better when **you** decide to step fully into who you were created to be.

With love and so much gratitude,

**Sandi Glandt**

# About the Author

## Sandi Glandt: High-Performance Productivity Coach, Author, and TV Host

Sandi Glandt is a high-performance productivity coach, best-selling author, Mrs. International 2022, and TV host on the CW's *Connect Network*. As a business owner, wife, and mom, Sandi understands the challenges of juggling a full plate, and she has made it her mission to help modern working women manage their time effectively. Through practical time-management strategies, she empowers women to take control of their schedules, prioritize what matters most, and transform overwhelm and burnout into focus and fulfillment.

Sandi is the author of the best-selling book *Slay Your Day: How to Get More Done, Become Ultra-Productive, and Unlock Your Full Potential!* and host of the *Slay Your Day* podcast. Each week, she shares actionable tips, tools, and insights to help her audience build thriving businesses, stay present with their families, and prioritize self-care.

Her clients consistently praise her for helping them turn their chaotic, busy lives into systems of massive productivity. They credit her guidance for creating the structure and clarity needed to effectively manage their time and achieve both professional and personal success.

Sandi proudly holds the distinguished title of Mrs. International 2022–2023, leveraging her global platform to champion the S3 Framework—Systems, Strategy, and

Support. Through this transformative methodology, along with her *Slay Your Day* book and signature programs, she empowers high-performing women worldwide to overcome burnout, reclaim their energy, and achieve sustainable success. As a sought-after speaker on international stages, Sandi is a leading voice in redefining modern productivity and wellness for today's working mothers.

Sandi lives in sunny Florida with her husband, Jarrod Glandt, and their two sons, Jacob and Jordan. As a family, they enjoy spending time at the beach, visiting water parks, and creating meaningful memories together.

**Here is how to connect with Sandi to maximize your experience:**

**Website:** https://www.sandraglandt.com/welcome
**Instagram:** https://www.instagram.com/sandiglandt
**Facebook:** https://www.facebook.com/SandiVGlandt/
**YouTube: https://www.youtube.com/@SandiGlandt**
**Blog:** https://businessandbody.com/

**FREE DOWNLOAD:** 5 Steps to Strategically Grow Your Business so You Can Work Less & Make More: https://www.sandraglandt.com/bigmoney

**BOOK:** Check out the number one best-selling book *Slay Your Day* here: ➡ https://www.sandraglandt.com/book

**Join the Productivity Hacks for Ambitious Women FREE Community TODAY:**
https://www.facebook.com/groups/382384305496676

Subscribe and listen to the *Slay Your Day* podcast here:
YT: https://www.youtube.com/@SandiGlandt

"You don't get what you want. You get what you decide you're available for. Choose abundance. Choose power. Choose the life you know you were made for."

— Unknown

"There is nothing too big, too bold, or too wild for the woman who knows her power and trusts her vision. The universe rises to meet her."

— Sandi Glandt

"I do not chase. I attract. What belongs to me will find me. and I show up every day as if it's already mine—because it is."

— Affirmation